ALLAN MORRISON is a prolific author; his previous books include *Last Tram tae Auchenshuggle!* which combines three of his passions: humour, nostalgia and Glasgow. His media appearances include The One Show, Richard and Judy and The Fred McAulay Show.

He is involved in charity work, after-dinner speaking and is a member of his local Rotary club. Allan enjoys hill-walking, sport and travel. He and his wife live in the West of Scotland and he is the proud grandfather of four grandchildren.

'Haud Ma Chips, Ah've Drapped The Wean!'

Glesca Grannies' Sayings, Patter and Advice

ALLAN MORRISON

Luath Press Limited
EDINBURGH
www.luath.co.uk

First published 2012
Reprinted 2012
Reprinted 2013

ISBN: 978-1-908373-47-2

The paper used in this book is recyclable. It is made
from low chlorine pulps produced in a low energy, low emissions manner
from renewable forests.

Printed and bound by
Martins the Printers, Berwick upon Tweed

Typeset in 10.5 point Sabon by
3btype.com

Contents

Introduction   7
Acknowledgements   11

Glesca Grannies' sayings, patter and advice about...

Appearance   13
Arguments   17
Blethering and Gossip   23
Children   29
Death   37
Discretion   41
Drink   45
Expressions   51
Family   59
Fashion   67
Food   75
Health   81
Home   89
Insults to Kith and Kin   93
Insults to Others   99
Money   105
Old Age   111
Problems and Worry   115
Sex, Marriage and Romance   119
Sports and Leisure   125
Temper   131
Useful Phrases for Daily Life   135
Weather   143
Wisdom   147
Work   155

Introduction

The only person capable of having an apparent mind-reader's ability to rootle around inside others' heads, is the typical Glasgow grandmother. Regardless of which part of the city they come from, they seem to have the ability to sum up situations and provide the appropriate advice. The dialect and accent may be slightly different depending on their social attributes and ambitions, but every last nuance of the rich communication is clear, creative and unambiguous. Many of the 'Glesca words' are self-evident in meaning. They are 'nearly-words', from the unique Glesca patois that is the currency of life in many a conversation. This book provides the many sayings and expressions favoured by grannies from Glasgow.

The reason is that Glesca grannies seem to have a God-given ability to be brilliantly observant and intuitive; a sort of hyper-intelligent, analytical creativeness that allows them to be continually alert to every foible of everyone's character.

But beware. They can also deliver their observations using cut-throat wit. Suddenly you can find yourself faced with an ace dragon, the crackle of her starched bosom confronting your face. So do not upset your typical Glesca granny or she'll have you pinned up against a wall like butterfly in a display cabinet.

On the other hand, Glesca grannies can be like grandmothers everywhere; transfixed by the machinations of the grandwean, and over the moon if they find out the wee darling will be the star of the school nativity play. In between strangulated mouthfuls of chips or water cress sandwiches, depending on their social standing, they will proudly proclaim to their friends about the amazing abilities of the fantastic wee souls that have clearly inherited something of the genes originally cooked up in her womb.

Improvisation is another major asset in the Glesca grannies' armoury. Never short of a word or six either to protect her offspring's offspring or to deal with an occasion when she feels that she has been slighted or taken for granted, or indeed to pass on a creative word of advice to a pal. 'A wee hauf o' valium an' a double vodka an' ye'll be as right as rain.' Or when, unusually, she has lost the thread of a conversation she might say, 'Haud ma chips, ah've drapped the wean!'.

Glesca grannies protect their grandchildren from the new evils of the world even if they themselves enjoy a whiff of the wicked weed occasionally. Some are even prepared, with grisly determination, to climb the rock face of alternative new strategies and move with the times in the bringing up of the little blighters.

Glesca grannies have lived through a remarkable evolution, not just in technology but also in social change. Now their level-headed pragmatic expressions, advice and sayings have been extended into the issues of today's society. Anyway, nowadays the compilation of the family unit can be an elaborately woven tapestry, so advice from this venerable authority needs to be as sharp as ever.

Many Glesca grannies may still have their original life companion with them, and by this time the old chap will have been well trained in the standards she expects of him.

If the original model of companionship has gone to the old man's hut in the clouds, then even although granny may lack the lithe, youthful suppleness of yesteryear, the war paint can still be applied once more. 'If that Nellie Whatshername roon the corner can get anither man then so by heavens can I.' So she may opt to join a gym, exercise or weight-reducing club, or indeed advertise her wares on the internet.

On the other hand, Granny may have concluded that the opposite sex is just an encumbrance and she is fed up with dirty socks, ironing shirts and an over-fondness for drink and football on the telly. So she will be content to be the family matriarch and ensure her grandchildren are brung up properly.

Acknowledgements

Many thanks to Ella Coventry, Val Grieve, Andrew Pearson, Ron and Anne Sheridan, Archie Wilson plus the number of Glesca grannies who kindly passed on their favourite sayings.

Appearance

'Ye've a dial oan ye like a well-skelped erse.'
You are certainly not a beauty.

'Yer face is fair trippin' ye.'
You are obviously upset about something.

'Ah need to get a new pair o' wallies fur this clapped-in dial o' mine.'
I could do with a new set of false teeth.

'Yer bahookie is o'er big.'
Your bottom is rather large.

'He's goat a face oan him like a torn melodeon.'

He looks miserable, like a broken accordion.

'Embarrassed! She had a big beamer.'

Boy, was her face red.

'She's goat a big bawface.'

Her face is large and full.

'There's no' twa pun o' her hingin the same way.'

She is far too fat.

'He's a right hard ticket.'

He is tough.

'She's goat a real crabbit face.'

She always looks as though she is in a bad mood.

'His face reminds me o' the back end o' a Glesca bus.'

He is not good looking.

Arguments

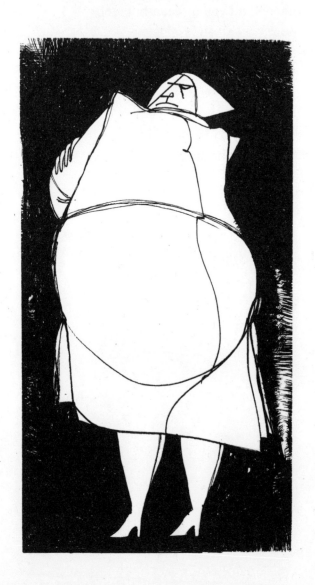

'Did sumbuddy banjo ye or jist gae ye a Glesca kiss?'

Did someone hit you or head-butt you?

'Whit's aw this kerfuffle?'

What is this commotion?

'Ah'm fair beelin' at you.'

I am extremely angry with you.

'Here, haud the jaikets.'
There is going to be a fight.

'Hing aboot, whit's the gemme?'
What is this all about?

'Ah'm fed up wi' the hale jing bang lot o' ye.'
You are all annoying me.

'Ye'r doin' ma heid in.'
Stop shouting and arguing.

'Hey, change the subject. We'll talk aboot turnips. Now, how's yer heid?'
You are an idiot.

'Whit's aw this palaver? Wan mere word oot o' you an' yer pan breid!'
One more word and you're dead!

'Behave yersell or ye'll get a bat in the mooth.'
Behave or I will give you a slap.

**'Pick brambles when they're ripe.
No' quarrels.'**
Don't say something you might regret at a later stage.

'They two had a square go.'
They had a fair fight.

'Ye'r nippin' ma heid.'

Stop complaining.

'Don't act it wi' me!'

Don't play the innocent with me.

'In a minute ye'll get yer heid in yer hauns tae play wi'.'

Behave, or else.

Blethering and Gossip

'She is the talk o' the steamie.'
Everybody is presently gossiping about her.

'Haud ma chips, ah've drapped the wean.'
I was not concentrating on what you were saying.

'Gie me a bit o' gossip any auld time... ah jist love it.'
I love a bit of scandal.

'See they so-called busy folk, believe me they are never o'er busy tae stop an' tell ye how busy they are.'
We all like to feel important.

'Don't be daft enough tae pit baith feet
in yer mooth at the same time,
or ye'll no' have a leg tae staun on.'

Watch what you say.

'Och, she's jist a know-it-all hairdresser who
wid make an equally guid taxi driver.'

She talks all the time and knows everyone's business.

'The folk who think they know it aw are
a real pain in the neck tae us lot that dae.'

There are some annoying 'know-alls' around.

'Some folks' gossip is so interesting ye almost
wish ye knew the person they wur talkin'
aboot.'

People enjoy hearing interesting tit-bits about others.

'Tell that wan nuffin'. She jist lets the chat oot the bag.'

That person cannot keep a secret.

'See tackless folk, they're jist sayin' whit everybody else's thinkin'.'

Some people just blurt out the truth of the matter.

'That lot think their eggs aw huv two yolks.'

They think they are superior.

'Believe me, that wan is a right warmer.'

That person is worth the watching.

'Ur ye payin' yer nosy club?'

Are you finding out what is going on?

'Thon's a bletherin' skite.'

That rather nasty person won't shut up.

'Away tae hell!'

You're surely kidding.

'Aye, right!'

That will be correct! Pull the other one.

'Ah believe anythin' if sumbuddy whispers it tae me.'

I tend to believe something if it's whispered in my ear.

'Away ye go!'

Wow!

'Wid ye believe it!'

That's amazing.

Children

'Ah wid bang yer heids thegither if it wisnae that the noise wid deafen me.'

You all need to behave.

'Och, that yin is no' the size o' tuppence-happenny.'

That one is very small.

'That wean's heid's wasted.'

That child is spoiled and seems to have a high opinion of themself.

'It's bucketing. Why have you jist got on yer sannies?'

It's raining and not a day to be wearing trainers.

'Did they get ye in a lucky bag?'

You are a bit different.

'"Amurnae" is no' the answer.'

'I am not' is not the answer I was looking for.

'Get yer hauns washed. They're boggin.'

Wash your dirty hands.

'Ah could hing oot ma washin' oan that petted lip.'

Don't give me that sulky look.

'Remember tae wash under yer oxters.'

Wash your armpits.

'She is jist a wee skelf o' a thing.'

She is small and skinny.

'If ye break yer legs don't come runnin' tae me.'

If you won't do what I tell you don't come and seek my sympathy.

'Ah'll gae ye somethin' tae cry fur in a minute.'

Behave yourself.

'The best time tae pit a wean tae bed is when they wull go.'

It is not easy getting some children to go to bed.

'Sure ye jist like tae sook in wi' yer granny?'

You like being my pal, don't you?

'See that wean, ah cannae be up tae him.'

You never know what that child will do next.

'Ye'r a wee bargain.'

We are lucky to have you.

'She's a right wee stoater.'

She is something special.

'An' jist who is 'she'? The cat's Auntie Peggy?'

Please do not call me 'she'. Call me by my name.

'Ah think they jist let ye hing as ye grow.'
I think your parents let you do what you like.

'Ye've jist given yer face a coo's lick.'
You have merely given your face a quick wipe.

'If ye keep plunkin' the schule ye'll never learn onythin''
You have to attend school to be educated.

'An' nae skidgin the schule, noo.'
Don't play truant.

Death

'Jist dae yer best fur ye urnae here o'er lang.'

Make the best of your life for, after all, life is over quickly.

'Aye, sadness hears the clock strike every hour but happiness forgets the day o' the month.'

Life is good until grief strikes.

'It's no' the pace o' life that ah'm worried aboot; it's the sudden stoap at the end.'

I am conscious that we are all mortal.

'Touch yer collar, touch yer knee, thank the Lord it isnae me.'

What granny told you to say when you saw a hearse.

'He jist woke up deid.'
He died in his sleep.

'Whit a sad funeral. It widda brought a tear tae a glass eye.'
It was very emotional.

'Wan mair clean shirt wull dae him.'
It will not be long before he dies.

Discretion

'Aw weans share chickenpox an' their mither's age.'

Children have no discretion.

'Tact closes yer mooth afore somebuddy else does it fur ye.'

Watch what you say.

'Listen you; never miss a chance tae shut up.'

Nobody would know there was anything wrong with you if you didn't open your mouth.

'Whit ye hear in yer ear can sometimes be heard a hunner miles away.'

It is surprising how stories get around.

'A sharp nose says yer a wee bit nosy,
an' a flattened nose says yer jist too nosy.'
Don't be over inquisitive.

'Never tap-dance in a wee boat.'
Be sensible.

'A wise man never laughs at his wife's
auld claes.'
A lack of discretion can be costly.

'The best way tae save face is to keep
the lower bit shut tight.'
If you don't talk then no one can criticize.

'Tell the truth an' ye don't need tae remember onythin'.'

It is better not to lie.

'Yawning might be bad manners... but at least it's an honest opinion.'

Body language can tell a lot.

'Ye don't insult Nessie till ye've crossed her loch.'

There is a time and place for everything.

Drink

'He taks a guid bucket.'

He is a heavy drinker.

'When the dram's inside the sense is ootside.'

Alcohol can make you lose your inhibitions.

'Some folks can end up pished wi' a right cargo.'

It is amazing how much some people can drink.

'Glad ah'm no' cleanin' oot his cage.'
He gets into a terrible state when drunk.

'Jist knock it back in a wanner.'
Drink it all at once.

'Ony mair o' this drink an' ah'll be blootered.'
If I drink any more I will be drunk.

'Naebuddy cares aboot yer accent as long as yer scotch is guid.'

Drink is important to a lot of people.

'A few haufs can change the colour o' the wallpaper.'

You see the world differently after drinking.

'He likes a wee snifter noo an' again.'

He drinks moderately and occasionally.

'A man taks a drink, the drink taks a drink,
the drink taks the man.'

Be careful that your life is not taken over by alcohol.

'Ah've seen him guttered a few times.'

Sometimes he is so drunk that he ends up lying
in the gutter.

'The big question is... does life begin at birth
or efter a couple o' haufs?

Whisky is enjoyable.

'Gae's a wee swally o' yer ginger.'
Give me a sip of your lemonade.

'Ah jist loved sugarallie-watter wance ah'd left it under the bed fur a week.'
I liked to drink water with liquorice in it after it had been kept in the dark for a week to mature.

'He is a bevvy merchant. Even likes the electric soup.'
He is a heavy drinker who also likes a mixture of fortified wine and methylated spirits.

'Jist the wan an' mak it a wee toaty wan.'
One small drink will do me.

Expressions

'Skedaddle aff!'

Away you go.

'Away an' birl your wilkies.'

Don't annoy me. Go and do something daft,
like a summersault.

'A'm away fur ma messages.'

I'm off shopping.

'Ah like a wee dauner roon the shops.'

I like walking around shops.

'Ah'm fair trachled the day goin' roon the shops.'

I am exhausted after shopping today.

'He's goat a heid like a stair heid.'

He is brainless.

'It's awfa nice to see folk wi' get-up-and-go, especially when they come tae visit ye.'

Do not overstay a welcome.

'Dae ye think ma heid buttons up the back?'

Do you think I am stupid?

'Och, yer jist bummin' yer chaff.'

You are showing off.

'Aye, an' yer granny's a cowboy.'
Don't be ridiculous.

'Not on yer bumbalery.'
You have no chance.

'That yin's a patter merchant.'
They are a smooth talking individual.

'Ah'm fair scunnered.'
I am feeling very turned off.

'Whit wis the best thing afore sliced breid?'
What else do you remember?

'Hey! Haud the bus a wee minute.'
Now, just hold on there.

'Ah'm black-affronted.'
I am deeply embarrassed.

'So who stole yer scone?'
Why are you unhappy?

'Wid it no' sicken yer humph?'
I am extremely disappointed.

'Jist wheech it up an' doon.'
Move that up and down.

'He's a right jammy dodger.'
He is a very lucky person.

'It wid sicken yer mince, so it wid.'
I am very disappointed.

'Maybe aye an' maybe hooch aye.'
I am doubtful.

'Missin' youse hunners.'
I'm missing you.

Family

'Today's weans wull have a job telling their weans whit they had tae dae withoot.'

I had to do without many things when growing up, but today's children seem to want for nothing.

'Ye don't limp jist because yer dug wis lame.'

Don't copy the bad habits of others.

'If the wummin had the first wean,
the man the second, the wummin the third,
believe me there wid be nae fourth.'

Men do not appreciate the traumas of childbirth.

'If ye sleep like a baby then ye sure ain't got wan.'

Babies can disturb your sleep.

'Cummere you. Ah've only got the wan hug left the day.'

Let me give you a hug.

'Hey, baith yer erms ur the same length.'

You have not contributed to this.

'Noo, remember an' no' gie me a riddy.'

Don't give me a red face.

'Ma grand-daughter thinks ah'm nosy. At least that's whit she says in her diary! Ha ha.'

I am an inquisitive person.

'Aye, an' folks wi' nae family bring them up right.'

People are experts when they only have themselves to consider.

'Ya wee dancer!'
You're really good.

'Whit's that up yer jooks?'
What have you got under your shirt or jumper?

'By the time yer children are fit tae live wi' ye they are usually livin' wi' sumbuddy else.'
It takes quite a while for some young people to mature.

'Wee hens learn fae big hens.'
You should copy me.

'When yer ship comes in ye'll probably be at Glesca airport.'
You will need to grow up and be smarter.

'Whit's yer face like fizz fur?'
Why are you annoyed?

'Ah'm no' exactly hard-hearted Hannah but ah'm no' a saft touch either.'
I am fair but strict.

'Hey, you're jist actin' it.'
You are being mischievous.

'Wake up! Ye'r in a dwam.'
Your thoughts seem to be elsewhere.

'They are gie scarce o' news that talks ill o' family.'
You do not discuss family affairs outside this house.

'That wan wid breastfeed her weans through the school railings.'
She spoils her family.

'Yer nose is aw snottery.'

Your nose is running.

'There's nothin' wrang wi' teenagers that arguing cannae mak worse.'

It is difficult for some teenagers to see sense.

'How come the loudest snorer is always the first wan tae sleep?'

Life can be unfair at times.

'Never lend anythin' tae onybuddy ye've given birth tae.'

Family can be careless with your possessions.

Fashion

'Believe me it's no' the skirt or troosers that maks a bum big.'

You have been overeating.

'Is the cat deid?'

Your clothes are too short.

'A corset is nothin' but a wee device to keep a bad situation fae spreading.'

Everything has its purposes.

'Yer dress reminds me o' a pelmet.'

Your skirt is too short.

'Ye've goat oan that jumper backside-furrit.'

You have your jumper on the wrong way round.

'A bonnie heid o' hair sells yer feet.'

Looking good influences people.

'Look at the ding o' that wan.'

That person is all dressed up and appears
to have a high opinion of herself.

'Whit have ye goat on yer trackies fur?'

Why are you wearing tracksuit bottoms?

'If ye ask me ye look a right haddie in that.'

You look silly the way you are dressed.

'They've taken it right intae the wid.
Ye've goat a baldie.'

The hairdresser has cut off too much of your hair.

'Yer claes are aw bumfled.'

Your clothes are creased and wrinkled.

'Och, ye look aw right. A blind man runnin'
fur a bus widnae notice anythin' wrang.'

You are acceptably dressed.

'Wummin may forget faces but they ne'er forget dresses.'
Ladies are very conscious of what other women are wearing.

'It used tae be wummin had bathing costumes doon tae their ankles. Noo they hardly wear baithies doon oan the beach.'
Ladies have become more daring.

'Ur ye goin' tae the hoor's ball?'
You are very skimpily dressed.

'Wid ye no' be better wi' a shed in yer hair?'
Why don't you have a parting in your hair?

'Sure it's great whit ye see when ye huvnae goat a gun.'
Just look at the way they're dressed.

'Jist look at that Teenie-fae-Troon.'
She is wearing an unusual outfit.

'Whit kind o' cadie is that?'
What kind of headwear is that?

**'Yer hair looks like straw hingin' oot
a midden.'**
Your hair is untidy.

'Yer grandpaw used tae huv a black tin flute.'
He had a black suit (probably for funerals).

Food

'Ne'er trust a skinny cook.'
They clearly don't eat their own meals.

'Watch ye don't slitter.'
Don't make a mess.

'Ah'm that hungry ah could eat a scabby heided dug!'
I'm starving.

'Ah wid jist love a Chick Murray.'
I would like a curry.

'Ye'll eat it afore it eats you.'

You will eat it whether you like it or not.

'See that wan, they wid eat anythin' that doesnae eat them first.'

They are not over fussy about what they eat.

'Never eat prunes when ye'r hungry.'

Otherwise you may find yourself making a number of visits to the 'small room'.

'Ah love fly cemeteries.'

I just love those cakes with a layer of currants between two pieces of pastry.

'Ah hate skittery wee helpings.'
I do not like small amounts of food on my plate.

'Help yersell. Ye're at yer auntie's.'
Please tuck into the food I have provided.

'Gie me a knickerbocker glory ony auld day.'
I love a mixture of ice-cream and fruit.

**'You've two choices. Eat yer dinner or leave it.
But see if ye leave it, ye'll get it fur yer tea.'**
Eat your meal!

'Aw yer gettin' is a run roon the table an' a kick at the cat.'

I am not telling you what you are having for the meal.

'Pick that up afore auld nick gie's it a lick.'

Pick up that food you have just dropped on the floor.

'Ah'm spittin' feathers.'

I'm very thirsty.

'That'll dae ye till ye get somethin' tae eat.'

That was a huge meal you just ate.

'Dae ye fancy a pokey hat?'
Would you like an ice-cream cone.

'Huv a jeely piece an' be done.'
After you have that sandwich you are getting' no more.

'Ah'll mak a clootie dumplin' fur yer birthday.'
I will make you a boiled dumpling in a cloth.

Health

'When dae ye get yer stookie aff?'
When will your plaster cast be removed?

'Ah'm fair pickled.'
I am somewhat unhappy with myself.

'Guid health is jist the slowest possible rate at which ye die.'
Keep healthy, but it won't stop you dying in the end.

'This is me since yesterday.'
I have been feeling like this for a couple of days.

'Keep away fae wacky-baccy.'

Don't touch cannabis.

'Dinnae cross yer eyes. Ye'll end up like that squinty bridge.'

Take care of your eyesight or you could get squinty like the Clyde Arc bridge.

'Och, arthuritis is jist twinges on yer hinges.'

Everybody gets aches and pains.

'He is corrie-fisted.'

He is left handed.

'That yin's no' goat a pick oan him.'
He is very thin.

'Ye don't wash yer dishcloots an' yer knickers thegither.'
You should observe good hygiene.

'Eat up, yer face is gettin' gey clapped-in.'
Your face is very thin.

'Ah hope it keeps up.'
You seem to be sniffing quite a bit.

'Ur you gonnae honk wi' a hoey?'

Are you going to be sick?

'Oor doctor couldnae cure a plouk oan a coo's erse.'

I don't think much of my doctor's abilities.

'A wee hauf o' valium an' a double vodka an' you'll be right as rain.'

A doubtful pick-me-up.

'Get in that shower. Ye'r mingin.'

You are dirty and smelly.

'Ah've cut doon oan the fags. Jist a wee dowt noo an' again.'

I only smoke half a cigarette or cigarette ends.

'The nurse gae'd me a wee jag.'

The nurse gave me an injection.

'The secret o' life is an aspirin a day, a wee dram an' nae sex oan Sundays.'

Some cheeky suggestions for a healthy life.

'Ma corns are fair loupin'.'

My corns are throbbing.

'Yer granpaw is oan the pat and mick.'

He is off work sick at the moment.

'Ah'm fair wabbit an' puggled.'

I am tired and out of breath.

'Ye'r lookin' a bit peelie wally.'

You are looking a bit pale.

**'Ye'll soon be able tae brush yer teeth
an' whistle at the same time.'**

Look after your teeth otherwise you'll require dentures.

'Ye'r getting' a bit malinky.'
You're becoming quite thin.

'Have ye no' washed? Ye'r reekin'.'
You are smelly.

Home

'This hoose is full o' oose.'
I need to do some cleaning.

'A Scotsman's hame is his hassle.'
Most problems start at home.

'Paddy's Market wis tidier than this place.'
This place reminds me of an old Glasgow street market.

'Ah wis brought up in a wally close, ye know.'

I lived in an upmarket tenement which had tiles on the close and stair walls.

'Oor neighbours have goat a sitterootery.'

They have a conservatory.

'Go an' see if next door wull gae ye a loan o' their macnamara.'

See if you can get a loan of their barrow.

'Ah like tae feed the chookiebirdies in the garden.'

I like to feed the birds.

'Get that windae closed. Ur ye tryin' tae heat Glesca?'

Close the window, you are wasting heat.

'This hoose is like Annacker's midden.'

This house is a habitual mess.

Insults to Kith and Kin

'See ma man, see his auld maw, see his granweans, see ma granweans, see chips an' gravy... cannae staun the hale lot o' them!'

I am disgruntled with all of you.

'Hell slap it intae ye!'

It's your own fault.

'Away an' lie in the midden!'

Get lost.

'Yer a gey nippy wee sweetie.'
You're very outspoken and awkward.

'Ya bampot!'
You're an idiot.

'Ye'r like a Christmas caird – aye greetin'.'
You never stop moaning.

'Yer heid's full o' mince.'
You are a right scatterbrain.

'That pit yer gas at a cheep.'
That fairly showed you up.

'Yer aw bum and parsley.'
You're full of yourself.

'Away an' bile yer heid.'
Get lost!

'Ye gie me the boak.'
You make me feel sick.

'Yer bum's oot the windae.'
You have no chance. You are talking rubbish.

'Away an' bite yer bum!'
Get lost!

'Yer a right strummel.'

You are a lazy idiot.

'Yer patter's like watter – it drips.'

You are talking nonsense.

'Ye've made a right coo's erse o' that.'

You have made a mess of what you were doing.

Insults to Others

'That lot ur jist two cheeks o' the same bum.'
They are all alike.

'They're a bunch o' doolies.'
They are all idiots.

'They're a lot o' big balloons.'
They are foolish people.

'That yin is a right wee toerag.'
He is despicable.

'He's nothin' but a greetin' faced wee nyaff.'

He is always moaning and groaning.

'That wan is goin' doolally.'

I think he is becoming a bit simple.

'Yon's a wee bachle.'

They are small and decrepit.

'He's a big dreepy-wullie.'

He has a woebegone expression all the time.

'That yin walks like a waggity wa'.'

The way they walk reminds me of a pendulum clock.

'If ye ask me he's no' the full whack.'

He is not totally in charge of his senses.

'That lot wid pit a tray under a cuckoo clock.'

They are not very bright.

'The only thing ye expect fae a pig is a grunt.'

They have low standards.

'Thon wid talk the teeth aff a saw.'
They cannot shut up.

'That yin is haun-knitted.'
They are a bumpkin.

'He's a right chookie.'
He is a silly person.

'Yer a right heidbanger.'
You are erratic and daft.

'He's a plumber oan his faither's side.'
He is certainly not a handyman.

'Goat a face oan him like a dug fae Govan wi' piles.'
He seems to be suffering.

'That yins goat a dial like a pun o' mince stuck in a door.'
They are not good looking.

Money

'Dae ye think ah'm related tae Carnegie?'

Do you think I have plenty of money?

'The guy who writes the telly ads for oor bank is certainly no' the man who gives oot the loans.'

It is quite hard to get a bank loan.

'That wan widnae gae ye a light in a dark corner.'

They are very mean.

'It's true that money talks. Mine says, "cheerio".'
My money doesn't last long.

'The only thing ye can dae oan a shoestring is trip.'
With limited money you have to be careful.

'Ah bought every hair in the tail.'
I paid too much for that.

'That lot are minted.'
They have plenty of money.

'Let me look in ma puggy.'
I'll look in my purse.

'Ah'm rooked.'
I have no money.

'Never lend money tae mates. It ruins their memory.'

Even friends sometimes forget to repay loans.

'Don't eat the lamb afore it's born.'

Don't spend what you do not have.

'No butter oan yer breid isnae poverty.'

At least you have bread.

'Ah'm jist aboot doon tae ma last thrupenny bit.'

I'm skint.

'Wan eye is worth the watchin'.'

If you don't have much money you should be very careful with what you have.

Old Age

'Dae ye think this is frost oan ma heid?'

I may be white haired and getting on a bit, but I'm not daft.

'It takes me mere time tae rest up than it does tae get tired.'

You have got to be realistic about your abilities when you are getting on a bit.

'Old age is jist the price we aw pay fur maturity'.

Older folks tend to have learned from life's experiences.

'Yer grandpa is pigeon chisted. That's why ah love him like ah do.'

He may have his faults but your grandfather is basically a good man.

'The aulder they get the better they were.'

Some tend to exaggerate their life's achievements as they grow older.

'Ah'm jist twenty-wan, an' ah wis born in nineteen-canteen.'

I'm not telling you my age.

'Sooner or later everybuddy's wild oats turns tae porridge.'

Age reduces libido.

'He is getting past it. Ye can tell by the way he jist wauchles aboot.'

He has started to shuffle.

Problems and Worry

'Ah've loast ma keys doon that stank.'

My keys have fallen down a drain.

'The ba's up oan the slates.'

Things have come to a head and we have a problem.

'He's fallen intae that sheuch.'

He has fallen into a ditch.

'Worry is like an auld rocking chair.
It gies ye somethin' tae dae but doesnae
get you ony place.'
Try not to worry.

'Be like an auld kettle. Even if it's up to its
neck in hot water, it still sings.'
Try to keep cheerful, regardless.

'Pit yer troubles in a pocket wi' a hole in it.'
Forget your problems.

'The only folks whose troubles are aw behind them are Glesca school bus drivers.'
Everybody has worries and concerns.

'Ah've been up tae high doh aw day.'
I am agitated.

'Is ma heart no' fair roastit?'
I am exasperated

Sex, Marriage
and Romance

'Treat yer wife like a thoroughbred
or ye'll end up wi' an auld nag.'
Have a good relationship with your partner.

'That wan suffers in silence louder than
onybuddy ah know.'
Believe me, she can let it rip at times.

'She should gie her man the heave.'
She should get rid of him.

'Ye don't really get ony 'huvtae cases' nooadays. The weans attend the wedding.'

There has been a change in what is acceptable in society.

'Mony a wifie should have stayed on her toes tae avoid a heel.'

Marry the right person.

'Plenty o' wummin marry a man fur life, then find oot he doesnae huv ony.'

You only really get to know a person well once you live with them.

'That yin jist goes roon kissin' mirrors.'
That person is only in love with themselves.

'Aw ah hear aboot is sexually transmitted diseases. Fur heaven's sake, life is sexually transmitted!'
Sometimes you forget the obvious.

'Ye wid never catch me knockin' aboot in the scuddy.'
I would never go around naked.

'Telling kids nooadays the facts o' life is like givin' fish a bath.'

Today children seem to know everything.

'Early tae bed, early tae rise, maks a man healthy, wealthy... an' the faither o' a big family.'

Everything has consequences.

'The moon disnae jist affect the tides ye know, it can stop caurs on dark roads.'

Romance and nature go hand in hand.

'When ah wis young the naughty girls went doon the dunny wi' the boys.'

Couples used to go down the stairs from the close mouth to the area under the tenement.

'Did ye get a knock-back at the club?'

Was your attention not appreciated by the opposite sex?

'She cawed the legs fae him.'

She swept him off his feet.

Sports and Leisure

'Noo, remember an' take a chitterin'
bite wi' ye if you go fur a wee dook
at the baths.'

Take some food with you when you go to the
swimming pool to eat after your swim in order
to prevent you getting cold.

'That wan couldnae hit a coo on the
backside wi' a banjo even if they wur
haudin' it by the tail.'

They are absolutely useless.

'The trouble wi' being a good sport is
tae prove it ye huv tae lose.'

Some things are annoying.

'That full back couldna tackle
a fish supper wi' salt an' vinegar oan it.'
That footballer is not good at tackling opponents.

'When ah wis young ah could jump
aff the dale.'
I used to jump off the high diving board at the
swimming pool.

'Most men don't care whit's oan the telly.
They only seem tae care whit else is oan
the telly.'
A lot of men like to continually channel hop.

**'When ah see him oan the telly
ah fair knot masell.'**

I cannot stop laughing at him.

**'Why dae the grannies in soaps look
aboot six months older than their weans?'**

Don't ask me questions I can't answer.

**'The only door oor telly opens is the
wan oan oor fridge.'**

Watching television can give rise to eating snacks.

'If ye must choose between two wee naughty wans, jist pick the wan ye've never tried afore.'

Have a wee shot at everything in life.

'We went tae the park but it wis hoachin' wi' folk.'

The park was very crowded.

'He's a rerr terr.'

He is a good laugh.

'Ask yer granpaw an' he'll gie ye a kerry-coal-bag.'

Granpaw will give you a fun lift on his back.

'Ye cannae touch me. Ah'm keys.'

I am taking a rest from this game.

'It will no' be lang till we're back tae auld claes an' purritch.'

Soon we will be back to our everyday lifestyle.

'He's awa oot oan the ran-dan.'

He is having a wild night out.

Temper

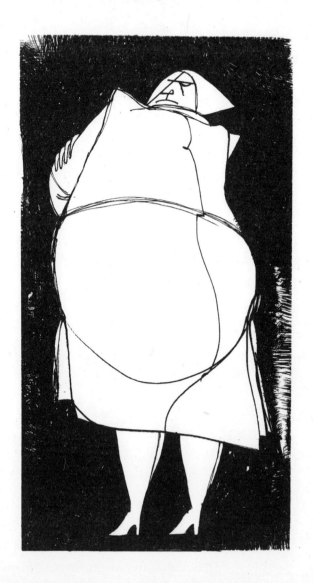

'Ah'm jist aboot tae lose the rag.'
I'm going to get angry.

'Don't you spit yer dummy oot at me.'
Don't you get angry with me.

**'Ah'm jist aboot tae huv an
Annie Rooney.'**
I am about to lose my temper.

'Behave, or ah'll no' miss an' hit the wa'.'

I will take decisive action if you don't behave.

'Ah'm gonnae go ma dinger in a wee minute.'

I am just about to lose my temper.

'Keep the heid.'

Do not lose your cool.

'Ah'm gonnae have a wee hissie.'
I am about to lose my temper.

'You deserve a right shirrakin.'
You need a telling off.

Useful Phrases
for Daily Life

'Gae it laldy!'
Do your best.

'Oh, ya beezer!'
That's just great.

'Gaun yersell, wee man.'
You can do it all by yourself. Keep going.

'Hey you! Heid-the-baw!'
Are you listening to me?

'Have a wee keek at this.'
Come and have a look at this.

'Ah huvnae a scoobie doo.'
I do not have a clue.

'Does yer mammy know yer oot?'
You are not on the ball today.

'It's worth hee haw.'
It is worthless.

'Ah've only a wee minute.'
Hurry up.

'Och, that'll be a skoosh.'

That is easy.

'Whit's oan the nock?'

What is the time?

'Ah widnae say eechie or ochie.'

I couldn't say yes or no.

'This year hameuldaeme.'

I will not be going away on holiday this year.

'Gonnae no' dae that!'

Please refrain from doing that again.

'If ah don't see you through the week ah'll see ye through the windae.'

I will see you later.

'The gemme's a bogie.'

We can't proceed.

'Away an' bile yer heid.'
Get lost.

'Ah'll share it oot eaksy-peaksy.'
I'll share it out equally.

'Oh, ya beauty!'
That's terrific.

'That's stonkin'.'
That is very good.

'Pure dead brilliant.'

That's just great.

'She talks pan loaf.'

She speaks with a posh accent.

'Intit no?'

Sure it is?

Weather

'Ye can moan as much as ye like but rain doesnae listen.'

Weather is something you cannot change.

'It's caulder than a brickie's bum.'

It's really chilly.

'It's gie dreich.'

It is a miserable, damp day.

'If you go oot ye'll get drookit.'

It is raining and you'll get soaked.

'It wid blaw the simmet aff ye.'

The wind today would even blow your vest off.

'It's Baltic in Glesca the day.'
It is extremely cold.

'That wind wid blaw aff snaw.'
The wind is fierce.

Wisdom

'Ah widnae go near that lot. They eat their young.'

They are a tough lot in that district.

'Behave or you'll go tae the bad fire.'

A hell of a scare tactic!

'A nail stickin' up gets hammered.'

Sometimes it pays to keep a low profile.

'They say it's good fur ye, but believe me there are only two kinds of pedestrians: the fast wans and the deid wans.'

Be careful when you are out.

'Shadows dinnae mak a noise.'

Always be on your guard.

'Jist stick in an' ye'll skate yer exams.'

If you work hard you will pass your exams.

'A used key disnae rust.'
Keep educating yourself.

'Only deid fish go wi' the flow.'
Don't be lead astray by others.

'Ye cannae swim oan the kitchen flair.'
Go and do that in the proper place.

'A biled egg is hard tae beat.'
You are stating the obvious.

'So, jist whit is the speed o' dark?'
You have just said something silly.

'If ye'r no' big enough tae stand a wee bit o' criticism, ye'r too wee tae be praised.'
Everyone gets praise and criticism in their life.

'Some o' these days he's goin' tae meet himsell comin' back.'
He is extremely clever.

'Don't blow oan dead embers.'
Forget the past.

'They've been like that since the lord left Partick.'
They have always been that way.

'It's better than a slap in the dial
wi' a wet haddie.'

It is better than nothing.

'Act daft an' get a free hurl.'

Some people appear simple but they are far from it.

'It's nae loss whit a freen gets.'

I may not have succeeded but at least you have.

'Aye, an' a day withoot light is called night.'
You are stating the obvious.

'Aye, an' virgin wool comes fae sheep that run the fastest.'
You certainly are kidding me.

'Lang may yer lum reek, an' may a wee moose never leave yer kitchen press wi' a tear in its ee.'
May you always keep warm and have food in your home.

Work

'Are you wan o' they high heid yins?'
Do you have a senior position at your employment?

'Ye'll need tae work harder or ye'll get yer jotters.'
You are in danger of being dismissed.

'That lot jist pey ye sweeties.'
Employees at that company are poorly paid.

'Aw ma life ah've had tae knock ma pan in.'
I've always had to work hard.

'Did the heid bummer gae ye the bag?'
Did the boss sack you?

'See folk that get on. They don't quit...
but quitters dae.'
Keep going regardless.

'Is yer jaiket oan a shoogly nail?'
Are you liable to be dismissed from your employment?

'Midges don't get a slap oan the back till they start work.'
You should work harder if you want praise.

'Heid doon, erse up.'
Concentrate on your work.

Luath Press Limited
committed to publishing well written books worth reading

LUATH PRESS takes its name from Robert Burns, whose little collie Luath (*Gael.*, swift or nimble) tripped up Jean Armour at a wedding and gave him the chance to speak to the woman who was to be his wife and the abiding love of his life. Burns called one of 'The Twa Dogs' Luath after Cuchullin's hunting dog in Ossian's *Fingal*. Luath Press was established in 1981 in the heart of Burns country, and now resides a few steps up the road from Burns' first lodgings on Edinburgh's Royal Mile.

Luath offers you distinctive writing with a hint of unexpected pleasures.

Most bookshops in the UK, the US, Canada, Australia, New Zealand and parts of Europe either carry our books in stock or can order them for you. To order direct from us, please send a £sterling cheque, postal order, international money order or your credit card details (number, address of cardholder and expiry date) to us at the address below. Please add post and packing as follows: UK – £1.00 per delivery address; overseas surface mail – £2.50 per delivery address; overseas airmail – £3.50 for the first book to each delivery address, plus £1.00 for each additional book by airmail to the same address. If your order is a gift, we will happily enclose your card or message at no extra charge.

Luath Press Limited
543/2 Castlehill
The Royal Mile
Edinburgh EH1 2ND
Scotland
Telephone: 0131 225 4326 (24 hours)
Fax: 0131 225 4324
email: sales@luath.co.uk
Website: www.luath.co.uk